Robert Adams

Wife Beating as a Crime and Its Relation to Taxation

read at a meeting of the Association, April 15th, 1886

Robert Adams

Wife Beating as a Crime and Its Relation to Taxation
read at a meeting of the Association, April 15th, 1886

ISBN/EAN: 9783337878641

Printed in Europe, USA, Canada, Australia, Japan

Cover: Foto ©Andreas Hilbeck / pixelio.de

More available books at **www.hansebooks.com**

PHILADELPHIA

SOCIAL SCIENCE ASSOCIATION.

Wife Beating as a Crime

AND

ITS RELATION TO TAXATION.

Read at a Meeting of the Association,

APRIL 18th, 1886,

BY

Hon. ROBERT ADAMS, Jr., A. M.

Bachelor of Finance, Wharton School.

Published by the
PHILADELPHIA SOCIAL SCIENCE ASSOCIATION,
720 Locust Street, Philadelphia.

WIFE BEATING AS A CRIME, AND ITS RELATION TO TAXATION.

During the session of the legislature of Pennsylvania, for 1885, a constit..ent put in my hands the following bill to be placed on the statue book :—

LEGISLATURE OF PENNSYLVANIA,

FILE OF THE SENATE,

No. 26, SESSION OF 1885.

Mr. Adams in place, January 16th, 1885.

Mr. Lee, judiciary, special, January 29th, 1885.

—. — — —

NEGATIVE RECOMMENDATION.

AN ACT

To provide for the infliction of corporal punishment upon all male persons convicted of wilfully beating their wives, and the manner and place of inflicting the said punishment, and the officers by whom the same is to be inflicted.

SECTION 1. Be it enacted by the Senate and House of Representatives of the Commonwealth of Pennsylvania in General Assembly met, and it is hereby enacted by the authority of the same, that whenever hereafter any male person shall wilfully beat, bruise or mutilate his wife, the court before whom such offender shall be tried and convicted, shall direct the infliction of corporal punishment upon such offender, to be laid upon his bare back to the number of lashes not exceeding thirty, by means of a whip or lash of suitable proportions and strength for the purpose of this act.

SECTION 2. The punishment provided in the first section of this act shall be inflicted by the sheriff of the county, or by one of his deputies within the prison inclosure, in the county

(3)

4

where the offence was committed, and in the presence of a duly
licensed physician or surgeon and of the keeper of the said
prison or one of his deputies, but in the presence of no other
person.

Upon a cursory examination I must frankly confess that
the act did not meet with my approval, and I introduced the
proposed law "by request," which is the formal way in which a
member disclaims personal responsibility. The bill was reported with a negative recommendation, but, in justice to my
constituent, I moved it be placed on the calendar notwith-
standing the adverse action of the committee. This is an unusual proceeding, and not often successful. The arguments
presented seemed to have some effect upon the Senate, or at
least upon its chivalric feelings, for it was so ordered upon the
calendar. The writer having thus championed the measure
prepared for the debate that was sure to ensue, and the result
of his studies led to a conviction of the wisdom of the proposed
law, as strong, as it had been luke-warm before. The bill
would undoubtedly have passed, had not the leaders of the two
parties for reasons best known to themselves, arrayed their
power against it. As it was, it received sixteen votes out of
the twenty-six votes necessery to pass it.

Many historians have agreed that the treatment of women
as a nation, is one of the best tests of its progress in civilization.
A short review will testify to the soundness of this conclusion.
In savage life, in which prowess alone commands distinction, the
comparative feebleness of women deprives her of recognition,
and she is the mere slave of man, for labor and drudgery. This
is equally true of the barbarians of the past, or the savage of
Brazil and North America of the present. The first idea of a
wife, seems to have arisen from the power to obtain and retain
possession of a woman. We read in the Bible of the capture of
wives from the daughters of the Shiloh, for the children of
Benjamin. The early history of the Greeks, Romans and He-
brews, is filled with expeditions made for no ostensible reason,

save that of procuring wives. Walter Scott says, that the Mac-Gregors captured a wife in 1750 for Robin Oig; a date so recent, that the deed might be set down to fiction, did we not know that it was necessary to pass a law in England in the third year of Henry VII. reign, making it a capital offence to carry away a woman without her consent. The next step in the matrimonial relation, was the sale of daughters among the semi-civilized tribes. This had the improvement of giving fathers and brothers some say in the disposition of the woman, and of at least rejecting brutal alliances. The Egyptians stand out in bold relief in respect to their treatment of women during the reign of the Pharoahs, but as their advanced state of civilization at that time is well known, it but adds a proof to the validity of the test before named.

The legal status of woman was changed early in the Greek law, and from that of a chattel to be sold, the father paid a sum of money to the bridegroom, which was the beginning of the custom of "dowry." This was secured to her, in case of separation, as well as an allowance from her husband, if he were the guilty cause of a divorce. Thus, a fixed legal status with personal rights was first given by Greek law. This raised her position in the marital state, and she became the companion instead of the plaything of the husband. The " Patria Potestas " of early Rome, gave absolute authority to the father over the family. He could sell his daughter to one of his own selection, and his authority was transferred to the husband as to the fortune and even the life of his wife. More mature Rome jurisprudence improved the status of the female, to the extent of inheritance of property and its retention independently of her husband. The fall of Rome and the institution of Feudalism, had a disastrous effect on the social and legal position of women. Martial service was the indispensible qualification of the right to hold property. Deprived of this, her personal rights were soon abridged. During the whole Anglo-saxon period, the law gave the power to the husband to exercise restraint by correcting her if necessary. Civil law allowed the husband for some misdemeanors "*flagellis et festibus acriter verberare uxorum*," and for others, only "*modicum castigationem adhibere.*" Au-

thorities do not agree as to what constituted a moderate casti-
gation, or the instrument wherewith it was to be inflicted.
Welsh law fixes as a proper allowance, "three blows with a
broom stick on any part of the body except the head." A
second law limits the size of the stick at the "length of the
husband's arm and the thickness of his middle finger." Another
rule was, that "a man may lawfully correct his wife with a stick
no bigger than his thumb." No wonder then, when Justice
Brooke, (12 Henry VIII., fol. 4,) affirms "that if a man beat
an outlaw, a traitor, a pagan, his villein or his wife, it is dis-
punishable, because by the law common, these persons can
have no action," he says "God send gentle women better sport
or better compane." But said Blackstone, in his Commen-
taries, "with us in the politer reign of Charles II. this power of
correction begins to be doubted, and a wife may now have security of the peace against her husband." "Yet the lower
rank of people who were always fond of the old common law,
still claim and exact their ancient privilege. It was not until
1829, that the act of Charles II., which embodied the old common law and allowed a man to "chastise his wife with any
reasonable instrument" was repealed.

The legal position of women, in this our century, is fully
established, so far as her rights to property are concerned, and
she is amply protected against her husband squandering her
wealth, be it real or personal. Her person itself occupies a less
secure position, and even the remedy offered by law, is not
available to her, owing to the attending consequences, and this
in spite of the constitution of the state, guaranteeing the right
of enjoying and defending life and liberty. The usual proceeding "in civiliter" of suit against her husband for damages
resulting from assault and battery, is denied her, owing to her
marital state, while the criminal prosecution, with the penalty
of imprisonment, deprives her of her children of needed support,
which anticipated result is frequently a bar to her even seeking
protection. The binding of her husband to keep the peace, or
the order of maintenance by the magistrate, has been found to
be futile, especially among the class to which most wife beaters
belong, namely :—drunkards, who are the only class allowed to

take the law in their own hands and inflict corporal punishment
on their wives for alleged faults, existing only too often in their
intoxicated brain, while fines and costs simply deprive the injured
mother, and innocent children of the necessities to sustain life.
Referring to the prevalence of the inhuman crime of wife beating, Darwin says, "with the exception of the seal, man is the
only animal in creation which maltreats its mate, or any female
of its own kind." Judicial statistics leave no question as to the
extent of the crime in England and Wales, issue of 1877, we
find that of aggravated assaults on women and children brought
under summary jurisdiction, there were reported in 1876, 2,737 ;
in 1875, 3,106 ; in 1874, 2,481, and of these it is estimated that
four-fifths were assaults made by husbands on their wives. It
is in centres of dense mercantile manufacturing and mining
populations, that this crime was most prevalent. In London
the largest returns for one year (Parliamentary reports of Brutal
Assaults) of brutal assaults on women were 351 ; in Lancashire
194 ; in Stafford, 113 ; West Riding, 15, and in Durham no
fewer than 267, with a population of only 508,666. In America
it has been impossible to secure any published statistics, but to
supply the place of such records, the following interrogatories
were sent to every district attorney in the State of Pennsylvania,
and their replies have been tabulated to show the results.

I. During the last year how many complaints were made
to the Grand Jury for wife beating, or for assault and battery
on wives by their husbands ?

II. How many true bills were found ?

III. How many convictions were obtained, and what was
the average term of sentence ?

IV. The nationality of the condemned ?

V. In your opinion is the crime on the increase ?

VI. Do you know if the families of the condemned, or
what proportion of them became a charge upon the county for
want of support ?

VII. Were the condemned under the influence of liquor,
at the time of committing the crime ?

Please return, etc.

[The table of returns will be found over leaf.]

525 brutal complaints by wives against their husbands for brutal beatings in one year is a terrible showing for a State so long settled and so far advanced in civilization in other respects as is Pennsylvania. 337 of the complaints were pronounced well founded by the grand jury, and 211 husbands were convicted for terms averaging three months each, thus depriving their families of necessary support. Would that we could flatter ourselves that these returns showed the full extent of this crime in our commonwealth, but it is probably ten times as great as is directly apparent. It will be noticed that there is no return from the coal regions of Luzerne County. Attention is also called to the prevalence of wife beating in Camden, N. J., which, except for geographical lines, is part of Philadelphia. The tabulated reports represent only the aggravated assaults, in which the wife driven to desperation by repeated assaults, seeks to have her husband imprisoned.

Hundreds of minor cases appear before the justices of the peace, or are settled before trial. This fact is established by the voluntary remarks of the several district attorneys. He, of Lycoming County, says: " The statement does not by any means represent the extent of the crime. Many prosecutions are settled before the justices that we never hear of. Many more wives are abused who will not make a complaint." The prosecutor of Northampton County says: " There probably have been many more such cases returned for trial during the year, but settled by parties before bill found. Many more have been settled by the justices of the peace and no returns made to court." Blair County: " I have had a great many cases of wife beating, but only some three or four have come to trial ; all generally settled and frequently before preliminary hearing." Montgomery County : " Desertion cases, which are disposed of on hearing without jury trial, develop a large amount of wife beating. These are not included in the queries. During the past year wife beating was developed in ten desertion cases." The District Attorney of Erie County says : " I find that a certain class of Englishmen beat their wives from habit." Dauphin County : " Only two specific charges of assault and battery

COUNTIES.	[During the last year, how many unmarried?]	How many true title were found?	[How long — term of sentence]	The Nationality of [the inmates]	[The persons who... for want of support]	[allowance of the families of the dwellers]	Were the individuals under the influence of ardent spirits when committed?	Notes.
Adams.			2	2 mos. and fines.	Americans.	None.	No.	No.	
Allegheny.	2	1, 2 years.	Not any.	90, 5 days to 1 year.	Irishman.	2.	No.	No.	Mostly.
Armstrong.							No.	No.	
Beaver.	Not any.						Yes.	No.	
Bedford.	4, 2.	10.	8.	3, fines and costs.	{4 Germans. 3 Irish. 1 English.}	1 or 2.	No. Yes.	1 or 2.	Yes. Yes. M were.
Berks.	4, 2.			1, 6 months.	American.		Yes.	2.	1 case.
Blair.	13.	None.		6, 2 days to 3 mon.	All.		Yes.		
Bradford.									
Bucks.									
Butler.									
Cambria.		1, 6 months.			German.		No.		Yes.
Cameron.	5.	1.		6, 30 days in a row.	{German. Irish.}		No. Ave.	No.	No.
Carbon.									
Centre.	3.		4, fines and costs.	{American. Irish.}	Yes?	No.	Not any.	Yes.
Chester.	5.		2, 6 years.	{German. German.}	Yes. No.		No.	
Clarion.									
Clearfield.	2.	2.	1, fines and fines.	{German. American.}	No.	None.	No.	Yes.
Clinton.				Cost and fines.			No.	No.	Yes.
Columbia.	None.	None.	None.	1, 2 months.	Colored.	No.	No.	Yes.
Crawford.	2.								
Cumberland.					Kerman.		No.	None.	
Dauphin.	1.		1, 1 year.	American.		Yes.		Yes.
Delaware.	New. Wid. Person. 3		None.		Germans.	No.	Xo.		Yes.
Elk.	None.	Some. None.	1, 6 months.	American.	Xo. Yes.	Vant.	No.	
Erie.	2.	2.	1, 30 days.	Americans.	Yes.	Yes.		
Fayette.	3, 4.	1, 30 days.	American.	No.	Do.		
Forest.	1, 1.	1, 6 months.	American.	No.		No.	No.	
Franklin.	4, 1, 6.	1, 30 days.	{German. German.}	No.	None.	No.	Yes. Yes.
Fulton.	7.	None.		American.		No.	No.	No.
Greene.	None.	8, 60 days.	{German. Irish and German.}	No.		Not any.	Yes.
Huntingdon.	12.			{American. Irish.}	No.	None.	No.	
Indiana.	4.	None.	6, 4, 15 days.	{Irish and American.}	No.	No.	Yes.
Jefferson.	10.		1, None.		No.	No.	Yes.
Juniata.	5, 2.	None.		American.		No.		Yes.
Lackawanna.	None.	9.	4, 3 months.	{Irish. English. Americans.}	Xo.	None.	Yes.	5 yrs. 4 mo.
Lancaster.	10.	6, 30 days, 6 mon.	{Irish. American.}	No.	No.	Yes.
Lawrence.	None.	No Record	No Record		No.	No.	Almost always.
Lebanon.	None.	182.	Xo, 5 months.	Indian. Americans.	Xo.	Not many.	Yes.
Lehigh.	2.	16.	15, 20 days.		Yes.		Yes.
Luzerne.	1, 3.	4, 1, 2 years, 6 mon.	American.	No. No.	None.	Yes.	3 yrs. 1 no. 1 mo. 1 yrs. 4 pts. 2 mo.
Lycoming.	Neat. None.	None.	Americans.	No.	None.		Yes.
McKean.	4.	None.	None.	{2 Welsh. 1 Irish.}	Yes.	None.	Yes.
Mercer.	4, 6.	1, 3 None.	Irish.		Yes.	None.	Yes.
Mifflin.	2.	3, None.	American.	No.	None.	No.	
Monroe.	None.	None.	None.	{Hungarian. Irish.}	No.		No.
Camden.	527.	125.	30, 15 to 60 days.	{Irish. American.}	30.	A few.	Yes. 20, no 7.	Mostly.

9

on wives, but in many desertion or maintenance cases, the testimony showed personal violence by husbands." Clearfield County reports : " Forty complaints have been made before magistrates in addition to complaints appearing in court." In the thickly settled mining regions of Schuylkill County, the preserver of the peace writes : " Thirty-six cases were returned by justices of the peace and were bound over by the judges for good behavior. Then we had about forty cases in which there was no trial from the fact that the wives asked the court to withdraw the prosecution of the defendant, as his imprisonment would leave the families in want." It is needless in order to establish the prevalence of this crime to quote from others who write in a similar strain.

Further, it will be noticed that wife beating exists to a greater extent, though not exclusively, among the foreign population, and it is certainly desirable that the baneful influence of the practice should be promptly checked before contaminating our native-born people.

To the question : " Were the condemned under the influence of liquor at the time of committing the crime ? " The answer is almost invariably in the affirmative. Here is a thought for those interested in the temperance cause. What effect would the whipping post have on these drunken brutes ? From eleven counties and from Camden comes the disheartening statement that in the opinion of the men best able to judge, the crime is on the increase.

Surely, with its prevalence in many counties and its increase in others, the present law is proved to be inadequate, and legislation is necessary on the subject.

The knowledge of the frequency of wife beating will be startling to the community, and the inadequacy of the present punishment evident. Infliction of punishment should always have a two-fold end—the reform of the criminal and the prevention of the committing of the crime by others. Hobbes says : " In revenges or punishments, man ought not to look at the greatness of the evil past, but the greatness of the good to follow, whereby we are forbidden to inflict punishment with any other design than for the conviction of the offender and the admonition of others." The latter has the greatest interest for the public for its own safety and that of its property.

The ordinary procedure, when complaint is made, is before justices of the peace, to whom the wife applies to have her husband bound over to keep the peace, or to provide maintenance. These cases are usually settled, the wife preferring to risk a second beating rather than deprive herself and offspring of food and shelter. The risk of such deprivation likewise deters the magistrate. The District Attorney of Cameron County writes: "The greatest difficulty in enforcing the law properly and punishing wife beaters arises from the fact that the wives themselves in every instance come into court and beg their husband's release. This has been my experience, and my predecessor says his was the same. Summary conviction before a magistrate and the whipping post within an hour after the crime would, in my opinion, be a good way to prevent the constant occurrence of this crime."

The District Attorney of Schuylkill County says: "There were about forty cases in which there was no trial, from the fact the wives asked the court to withdraw the prosecution. To imprison the defendant would only leave their families in want."

The District Attorney of Lycoming County testifies: "Except in aggravated cases, settlement is encouraged because the parties are all poor and have no money for the costs and fines, and their families suffer while they are in prison."

The District Attorney of Pittsburgh writes: "In most cases the wives come into court and beg for the release of their husbands."

The District Attorney of Philadelphia says: "I have no doubt the imprisonment of the wife beater in a large majority of cases causes very great suffering to the innocent families. More indeed than his incarceration inflicts on him."

In the more formal and protracted procedure of complaint and indictment by the grand jury, followed by trial in court, the objections noted rise to even a greater degree of force, and Judge Mitchell of Philadelphia, informs the writer that, in cases in which conviction has been had he has invariably been appealed to by the wife to impose only a short sentence, as long imprisonment meant starvation to the family of the convicted.

Confinement in the county jail, where not even hard labor is imposed, has no terror for a brute so demoralized that he will strike a woman—his physical inferior, and by nature he is incapable of feeling for those suffering at home.

It has been urged that wives would not inform on their husbands and expose them to the disgrace of being whipped. But at least they would have a chance, and it will be seen from the testimony given that the law as at present existent does not even give them any option, for with the want of food staring them in the face, they dare not complain. The punishment of the lash is not open to the objection that want will follow to the complainants, and if they have a remedy and prefer to suffer, it is for them to decide. Wife beating is not done openly where the law can see and take cognizance of the breach of the peace, and that the law may be put in motion it is essential that the wife should be placed in an untramelled position, free to protect herself by making complaint.

There is an economic side to the whole matter which affects the community far more than the mere horror of the brutality of the offence. Society is an organization to protect itself. The combining of the weaker against the strong, and the employment of the machinery of the law offers comparative safety to the individual. To sustain the system society is willing to be taxed ; to have prisons built ; judges and prosecuting attorneys paid ; police hired ; convicts immured and supported, and for every murderer hung or incarcerated, the sense of increased security for his person is a return to the individual for the tax paid, and the conviction of each thief is a consideration received on account of the premium paid for the security of property.

What relation does the crime of wife beating bear to the taxpayer beyond the shock to his feelings of humanity? It affects the citizen in *no degree* if the brute plies his vocation every day of the year. The person of the taxpayer, if anything,

is less secure, for the brute from force of habit in inflicting pain
might assault others who were his physical inferiors, while the
property of the taxpayer, if the brute is convicted and sentenced,
is taxed to support him in jail. The evil does not end here, for
the chances are largely in favor of the wife and children of the
criminal being left a charge on the county as inmates of alms-
houses during his imprisonment. The number of persons who
thus become a charge upon the county, it is next to impossible
to estimate. In reply to the inquiry on this subject the several
district attorneys were unable to give information save in a few
cases, and as commitments only read "assault and battery," no
information can be gleaned from the prison registers.

The men convicted of this crime are married, and with the
average family, the number of persons deprived of support can
not be small. The incomplete returns give 211 convictions
with an average sentence of three months each, which at twenty-
five cents per diem, makes a charge upon the taxpayer of over
$5,000 annually for supporting these brutes in idleness. Not a
pleasant thought certainly. Of course the subject might be
pursued further in this direction, and we might discuss as a
matter of loss to the State the pay of jurors, witness fees, also
the time wasted by courts and attorneys in trials of wife beaters
while important civil cases awaited adjudication. An additional
loss is the money spent in the purchase of the alcoholic stimu-
lant with which these brave men fortify themselves for the
heroic deed of attacking their wives—their physical inferiors, to
say nothing of the further loss due to the habit of idleness ac-
quired during their imprisonment without labor. But enough
has been adduced to support, from an economic view, the passage of a law to suppress this crime.

In a recent debate in the Senate of Pennsylvania objection was raised by a Senator, not trained in the law, that the
proposed punishment was in violation of the constitutions of the
United States, and of this commonwealth. The amendment to
the constitution of the United States, forbids "cruel and *unusual* punishment." This is a restriction of the Federal govern-
ment, and not upon the States. It is inapplicable to offences

against the State. This is well recognized, and has been adjudicated in the case of Barker *vs.* The People, 3 Cow, (N. Y.) 686. The law as it existed in the Slave States formerly, and as it exists in Delaware and Maryland to-day, is a sufficient answer to the objection. It will be noticed that the constitution of Pennsylvania, does not retain the wording of the bill of rights, 1st., Wm. and M., as does the constitution of the United States, but omits the word *unusual.* That this omission was designed by the framers, there can be no question, as to the original phrasing was of too ancient a date, and too familiar to be mistaken, and formed one of the most pronounced declarations of that statute which established security of personal liberty. In interpreting the portion of the bill of rights cited, James Fitzjames Stephens says, "no doubt the flogging of Oats, and others who were sentenced, were the cruel punishments which parliament referred to." Macauley in describing the infliction of the sentence, says, that Oats was expected to die. He was whipped twice at an interval of two days. "The hangman" "laid on the lash with such unusual severity, as showed that he had received special instructions. The blood ran in rivulets." On the second whipping he received 1700 lashes. It was the prevention of such cruel and unusual punishment as this, that the provision of the bill of rights was directed, and not against whipping itself. This is substantiated by the fact that "whipping has never been formally abolished for common law misdemeanors," (Stephens) but on the contrary, has been named as punishment to be inflicted in the acts 26 and 27 Victoria C 44, where the number of whippings, and the instrument to be used, and the number of strokes to be inflicted, are set forth In 1863, this statute, the Garroters, Act was passed by parliament, discretionary power being given to the judge, to inflict the additional punishment of flogging, and this most atrocious crime of strangling, which had held London in terror for several years disappeared after one or two convictions.

These statutes plainly show, that in England the section of the bill of rights against cruel and unusual punishments is held not to refer to whipping properly administered as a punishment.

In Pennsylvania up to the time of the adoption of the constitution of 1790, in which was first inserted the restriction against cruel punishment, the provisions of the first, Wm. and M. were in force, and to show that the interpretation in this state was the same as that in England, I cite the act of March 10, 1780, (first Smith's laws 501) in which punishment for horse stealing is prescribed. " Every such person or persons so offending, for the first offence, the offender shall stand in the pillory for one hour, and shall be publicly whipped on his or on their bare back with thirty-nine lashes well laid on." And the act of March 16, 1785, prescribes, that for counterfeiting, the offender " shall be sentenced to the pillory, to have both his or her ears cut off and nailed to the pillory." These were not considered cruel and unusual punishments, under the bill of rights, nor can they be held to be in violation of the clause of the constitution of 1790, for they remained statutes after its adoption for nearly fifty years, and were only repealed by the act of April 3, 1829, although it may be a question as to what was the effect on this subject of the acts of April 5, 1790, and April 22, 1794. The present constitution of Pennsylvania retains the clause of the former constitution, verbatim, in regard to cruel punishment, and as the case is in no wise changed, I hold that there is no constitutional prohibition preventing the passage of the law inflicting whipping as a punishment.

It has long been debated whether flagellation as a punishment or flagellation as a penance, was the more ancient of the two kinds of whippings ; but the Rev. Wm. M. Cooper, in his history of the Rod, decides that corporal punishment is as old as sin, and that voluntary flagellation was in imitation of punishment inflicted on themselves, by those feeling guilty of such sins as they had committed. That whipping is one, if not the oldest mode of punishment, history offers ample proof. In Exodus, we read that Pharoah flagellated the Israelites. In the laws of Moses, flagellation was imposed for certain offences, the number of lashes being limited to forty. Jesus Christ was scourged before crucifixion. The Romans carried the practice of flagelletion further perhaps, than any other nation. Horace tells of the nicety to which it was administered in his accounts of the " Ferula, the Scutica, and the terrible Flagellum." The celebrated cases of Henry II. in England, and Miss Cadiere in France, suffice, as examples of the middle ages, while Austria, Russia, China, Turkey and Siam, at the present day, apply the rod in various forms as a means of punishment. But it is far from the object of this paper, to advocate whipping as a punishment in general, or to approve the law as it exists in the state of Delaware to-day. The object is only to urge whipping, as a remedy for the crime of wife beating, and in so urging I am in consonance with the doctrine laid down by James Fitzjames Stephens, the ablest judge that ever set in an English criminal court, and one of the most learned writers on criminal law. In his History he says, "the view which I take of the subject, would involve the increased use of physical pain, by flogging or otherwise by way of secondary punishment. It should, I think, be capable of being employed at the discretion of the judge, in all cases in which the offence involves, cruelty in the way of inflicting pain, or in which the offenders motive is lust. In each of these cases the infliction of pain is what Benthan calls a 'characteristic punishment.' The men who cruelly inflicts pain on another, is made to feel what it is like. The man who gratifies his own passions, at the expense of cruel and humiliating insult inflicted on another, is most fearfully and shamefully humiliated." In 1874 the home office of England issued a circular requesting opinions, whether flogging should be authorized in cases of assault, especially on women and children. There was a great unanimity of opinion, that the law as it stood was insufficient, and that the penalty of flogging should be added to the list of sanctions. Lord Chief Justice Cockburn, Justices Blackburn, Meller, Lush, Quain, Archibald, Brett Grove, Lord Chief Baron Kelly, and Barons Bramwell, Piggott, Pollock, Cleasby and Amphlet were all of this opinion. Lord Coleridge and Mr. Justice Denman were hesitating, and Mr. Justice Keating, of all who sat upon the Bench, was the only opponent of flogging. The chairman and Magistrates in Sessions, were in sixty-four cases out of sixty-eight, in favor of

16

whipping. The Recorders of forty-one towns were likewise in favor of it, only three entering their protest against it. In our own Commonwealth, the subject has been but too recently agitated, to arouse any public opinion. When at the last session of the legislature, a bill to establish the whipping-post for wife beaters, was introduced in the Senate by the writer, he was flooded with letters from within and without the state, in support of the bill, and copies thereof asked for, even from Canada. The proposed act received the almost unanimous support of the public press. In he interrogatories sent to the several district attorneys, the direct question of their opinion as to the establishment of the whipping post as a punishment, was not asked for two reasons : First, in the agricultural counties, the crime exists to a slight extent only, and the attorneys, probably in ignorance of its prevalence elsewhere, would naturally see on necessity for it. In the second place, the reasons for imposing whipping as a punishment, solely for the crime of wife beating, have but recently been given to the public. The following *voluntary* remarks, therefore, have double force as spontaneous opinions of the public prosecutors, The District Attorney of Schuylkill County, says "there is a growing sentiment in this county in favor of your bill. Our judge has spoken favorably of it, and reminded a defendent as he was about to sentence him, that *he* hoped that the day was not distant when wife beaters, would be punished as directed in your bill." The District Attorney of Westmoreland County adds : "as a rule the same parties in a year or so, turn up in court again for the same offence. The whipping post is the only adequate punishment for the offence." The District Attorney for Cameron County testifies, "the law in its present condition, is utterly powerless to prevent this crime. Summary conviction before a magistrate, and the whipping post within an hour after the crime, would in my opinion be a good way to prevent its reoccurrence." The District Attorney of Adams County, puts a P. S., "your proposed correction of this evil, when the case is clearly established, meets with my hearty approval." Forest County : "A law to flog wife beaters would be good." The judgment of the District Attorney of Bradford is, "we ought to have the old whipping post in Pennsylvania, and nothing else will so effectually check this most dastardly crime." The District Attorney of Franklin, writes: "I heartily favor the whipping post." Clearfield County, represented by District Attorney, says, "in the writer's opinion, the Delaware whipping post would be a salutary preventative for this crime." The opinion of the experienced District Attorney of Philadelphia, who presented 308 bills to the Grand Jury, and convicted eighty brutes of this cowardly crime, is "in my judgment, the re-establishment of the whipping post or some mode of corporal punishment inflicted privately, would be more effective to reduce the number of wife beaters than the punishment of incarceration." Three Grand Jurys of Philadelphia County, recommended the passage of this bill to the legislature, and four called the attention of the public to the prevalence of the crime. The opinions of the Judges of the Court of Common Pleas of the State, on the advisability of whipping as a remedy for wife beating, are generally unknown to the writer, but the mature judgement of the two judges longest in service on the Philadelphia Bench, Judge Allison,—and Judge Ludlow is junior but a few years,—both favor the proposed punishment.

It is a curious fact that the Code of Delaware, which inflicts whipping for so many crimes, does not impose it for the offence of wife beating. We can therefore get no information from Delaware as to the efficacy of whipping in suppressing and preventing this particular crime, however potent it may be against others in that state.

In 1883 the Legislature of Maryland passed a bill to punish wife beaters by whipping them, and the District Attorney of Baltimore informed the writer that after the first conviction the crime ceased as if by magic, in that state. With this last unanswerable testimony, the writer closed his argument in favor of the establishment of the whipping post for the offence of wife beating, feeling fully persuaded that the sentiment which undoubtedly exists to a certain extent against whipping as a punishment, will, as did his own individual feeling, change when the facts are known, and when it is well understood that corporal punishment is to be inflicted solely in cases of wife beating.

THE FOLLOWING IS A LIST OF THE PAPERS READ
BEFORE THE ASSOCIATION.

1871. *Compulsory Education.* By Lorin Blodget. *
Arbitration as a Remedy for Strikes. By Eckley B. Coxe. *
The Revised Statutes of Pennsylvania. By R. C. McMurtrie. *
Local Taxation. By Thomas Cochran. *
Infant Mortality. By Dr. J. S. Parry. *

1872. *Statute Law and Common Law, and the Proposed Revision in Pennsylvania.* By E. Spencer Miller. †
Apprenticeship. By James S. Whitney.
The Proposed Amendments to the Constitution of Pennsylvania. By Francis Jordan.
Vaccination. By Dr. J. S. Parry. *
The Census. By Lorin Blodget. *

1873. *The Tax System of Pennsylvania.* By Cyrus Elder. *
The Work of the Constitutional Convention. By A. Sydney Biddle.
What shall Philadelphia do with its Paupers? By Dr. Isaac Ray.
Proportional Representation. By S. Dana Horton.
Statistics Relating to the Births, Deaths, Marriages, etc., in Philadelphia. By John Stockton-Hough, M. D.
On the Value of Original Scientific Research. By Dr. Ruschenberger.
On the Relative Influence of City and Country Life, on Morality, Health, Fecundity, Longevity and Mortality. By John Stockton-Hough, M. D.

1874. *The Public School System of Philadelphia.* By James S. Whitney.
The Utility of Governmemt Geological Surveys. Professor J. P. Lesley.
The Law of Partnership. By J. G. Rosengarten. *
Methods of Valuation of Real Estate for Taxation. By Thomas Cochran.
The Merits of Cremation. By Persifor Frazer, Jr.
Outlines of Penology. By Joseph R. Chandler.

1875. *Brain Desease and Modern Living.* By Dr. Isaac Ray. †
Hygiene of the Eye, Considered with Reference to the Children in our Schools. By Dr. F. D. Castle.
The Relative Morals of City and Country. By William S. Pierce.
Silk Culture and Home Industry. By Dr. Samuel Chamberlaine.
Mind Reading, etc. By Persifor Frazer, Jr.
Legal Status of Married Women in Pennsylvania. By N. D. Miller.
The Revised Status of the United States. By Lorin Blodget.

1876. *Training Nurses for the Sick.* By John H. Packard, M. D.
The Advantages of the Co-operative Feature of Building Associations. By Edmund Wrigley.
The Operations of our Building Associations. By Joseph I. Doran.
Wisdom in Charity. By Rev. Charles G. Ames. *

1877. *Free Coinage and a Self-Adjusting Ratio.* By Thomas Balch.
Building Systems for Great Cities. By Lorin Blodget.
Metric System. By Persifor Frazer, Jr.

1878. *Cause and Cure of Hard Times.* By R. J. Wright.
House-Drainage and Sewerage. By George E. Waring, Jr.
A Plea for a State Board of Health. By Benjamin Lee, M. D.
The Germ Theory of Disease, and its Present Bearing upon Public and Personal Hygiene. By Joseph G. Richardson, M. D.

.

www.ingramcontent.com/pod-product-compliance
Lightning Source LLC
Chambersburg PA
CBHW021611270326
41931CB00009B/1425